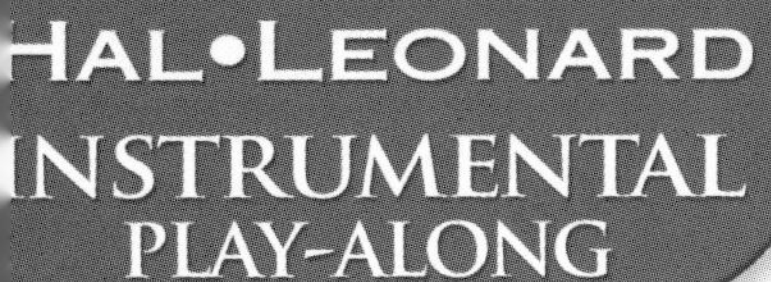

CELLO

TOP HITS

Audio arrangements by Peter Deneff

To access audio visit:
www.halleonard.com/mylibrary

Enter Code
5370-5481-2007-7223

ISBN 978-1-4950-6581-1

7777 W. Bluemound Rd. P.O. Box 13819 Milwaukee, WI 53213

Visit Hal Leonard Online at
www.halleonard.com

ADVENTURE OF A LIFETIME

CELLO

Words and Music by GUY BERRYMAN, JON BUCKLAND, CHRIS MARTIN, WILL CHAMPION, MIKKEL ERIKSEN and TOR HERMANSEN

BUDAPEST

CELLO

Words and Music by GEORGE BARNETT
and JOEL POTT

To Coda
D.S. al Coda
(no repeat)
CODA
mf

DIE A HAPPY MAN

CELLO

Words and Music by THOMAS RHETT,
JOE SPARGUR and SEAN DOUGLAS

To Coda
7
D.S. al Coda
CODA
mf
mp
rit.

EX'S & OH'S

CELLO

Words and Music by TANNER SCHNEIDER
and DAVE BASSETT

To Coda
3
D.S. al Coda
CODA
3
3
7
mf
f
1.
2.
3
3

FIGHT SONG

CELLO

Words and Music by RACHEL PLATTEN and DAVE BASSETT

1.
2.
D.S. al Coda
CODA
mp
2
mf
f
mp rit.

HELLO

CELLO

Words and Music by ADELE ADKINS
and GREG KURSTIN

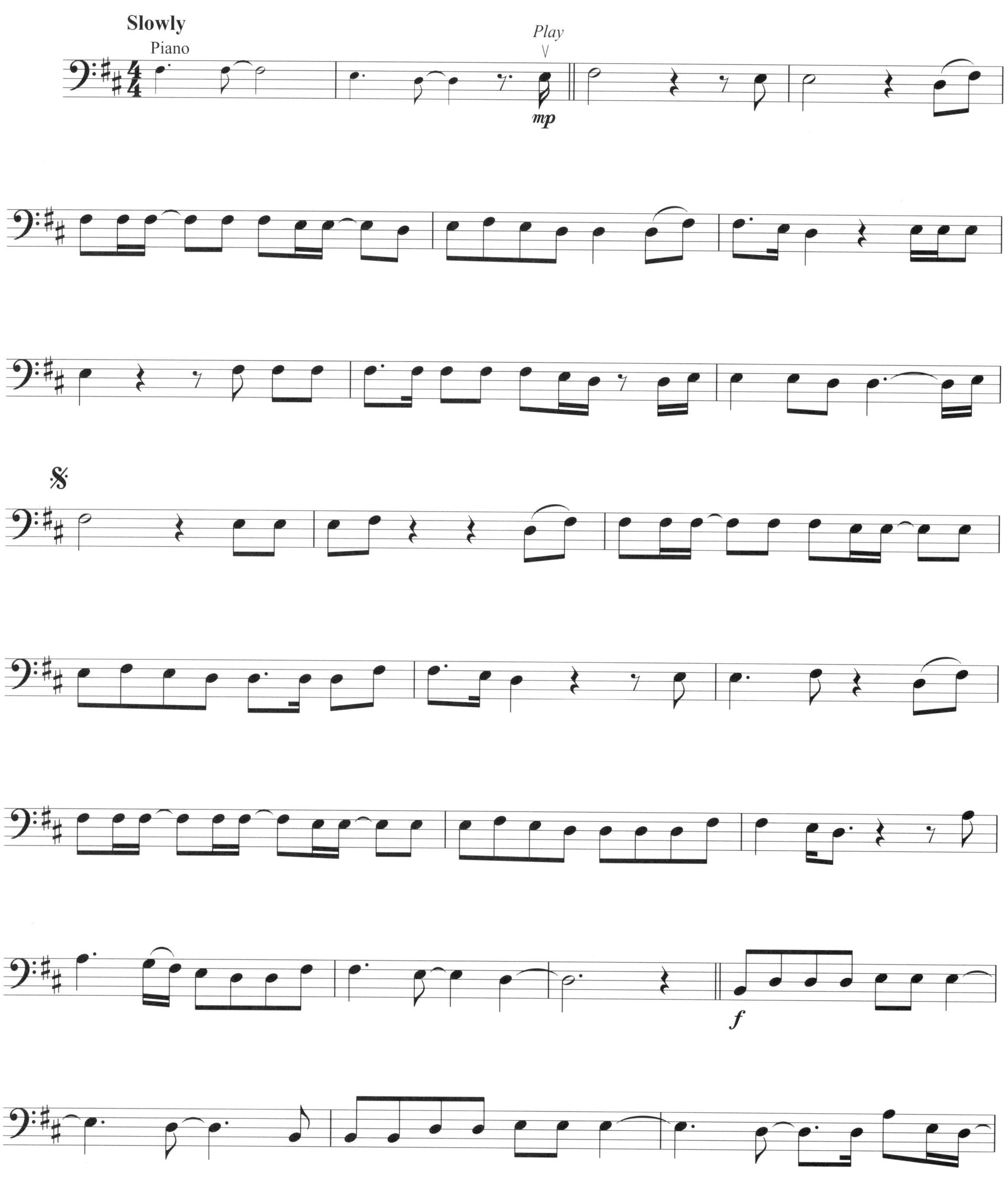

f
To Coda
D.S. al Coda
mp
CODA
1.
2.

LET IT GO

CELLO

Words and Music by JAMES BAY
and PAUL BARRY

2.
To Coda
7
D.S. al Coda
CODA
7
mf
1.
2.
mp
1.
f
2.
8

LOVE YOURSELF

CELLO

Words and Music by JUSTIN BIEBER,
BENJAMIN LEVIN and ED SHEERAN

f
1.
2.
8
mf
f
1.
2.

ONE CALL AWAY

CELLO

Words and Music by CHARLIE PUTH,
BREYAN ISAAC, MATT PRIME,
JUSTIN FRANKS, BLAKE ANTHONY CARTER
and MAUREEN McDONALD

f
mp
1.
f
2.
mf
rit.

PILLOWTALK

CELLO

Words and Music by LEVI LENNOX,
ANTHONY HANNIDES, MICHAEL HANNIDES,
ZAYN MALIK and JOE GARRETT

To Coda
D.S. al Coda
(take 3rd ending)
CODA
3
3
3

STITCHES

CELLO

Words and Music by TEDDY GEIGER,
DANNY PARKER and DANIEL KYRIAKIDES

To Coda
D.S. al Coda
CODA
4
1.
2.

WRITING'S ON THE WALL

from the film SPECTRE

CELLO

Words and Music by SAM SMITH
and JAMES NAPIER